NAKED SOUL:

THE EROTIC LOVE POEMS

Naked Soul:

The Erotic Love Poems

Salil Jha

Naked Soul Press

NAKED SOUL: THE EROTIC LOVE POEMS

Printed in United States of America

ISBN: 0692265295
ISBN 13: 9780692265291
Library of Congress Control Number: 2014913781

First Edition: December 2014

Naked Soul Press
Quincy, MA 02171

Neha

The sweetest, most loving heart I have ever known.
What I have in you is what every
person in the world is searching for.

Contents

PREFACE

Naked Soul: The Erotic Love Poems is a beautiful collection spanning a wealth of human emotions and dealing with the themes of love, romance, chase, seduction, and sensuality. The poems here cover topics ranging from spiritual love to ecstatic joy, from strong passion to sweet seduction, from first love sensations to a lover's longing, from conservative and familiar love to inhibited erotic fantasies.

The words here are not just poetic but sublime, touching the heart, gently massaging it with visual imagery, metaphor, and emotionally explicit, innocent, intimate expressions.

Most of the books of erotic poetry available today are either too old or are big anthologies covering the same poets and poems. There is a lack of new and original work. Most of us have read something from Ovid, Sappho, Shakespeare, the ancient Greeks, the Romans, or from the *Kama Sutra*. But love is a theme that should be celebrated with freshness.

There is too much noise and stress out there in the world. Chances are if you are reading this book, you have an artist in you. You are a reader, and therefore a thinker, an observer, a living soul who wants more out of this human experience. The reader of these poems can relax while slowly reading, reflecting, and visualizing what it would be like to make love with his or her beloved (or a fantasy figure). This book is full of poems—everyday stories we can all relate to.

Poetry contains few words but tells much. Its beauty is that by being condensed it is rich in meaning and open to various interpretations. Unlike prose, there is no boundary to poetry. There is nothing concrete or black and white. Poetry is mutable; it is transformative. Poetry is the alchemy of hearts. And what cannot be said in prose can sometimes be only said through poetry. Poems are word paintings. Poetry doesn't belong to time. That's why often you feel as if poems are speaking directly to you.

This book's theme is vast: romantic, sacred, symbolic, vivid, happy, lighthearted, and erotic. Some poems are very rhythmic while some are written in free verse. Any poetry lover who loves deep symbolism, storytelling, and musing over deep verses will find this book very touching. Read it slowly. Read a poem at a time, or two, or all, but give them time to sink into your heart. Read them again, read a portion, and stop and ponder. Visualize. Take it slow; let the poem show you what lies in your own heart. Let it fuel the words from within.

Let your heart speak its own poetry and feelings. Let your desire be touched by these words. Let these poems stir the passion in you. Once this passion is aroused and strengthened, you will live in the moment, fearing nothing, living for no one but your own soul and the duty that it has carried since the time of your birth. This book is all about getting in tune with our deepest, most intimate feelings.

Every soul needs a touch of erotic love. A deep, unconditional love is what every heart truly desires. True love is passionately erotic.

These are not ordinary poems. These are the expression of eros that cannot be said but still has to be said. You can sing it, but you cannot say it; you can dance to it, but you cannot explain it. You can see it in the poems even though I cannot show it to you by my words. Just feel the words because these poems are written not to be understood by the mind but to be felt by the heart.

These are love poems for every mood and sentimental feeling. No matter which phase of love you are growing in currently, this book will serve to sail you further toward the endless ocean of love. May this collection add to our lives and enrich the depths of our relationships. May all of us be fully saturated by the all-consuming force of love.

Salil Jha
Boston, MA

BRIEF INTRODUCTION

Every poem is unique to each person who reads it.

Readers holding this book must know that what they possess in their hands is not an ordinary poetry book. This book is a deep poetic musing at the soul level. The love poems that you'll read on the following pages possess the erotic spirit of humankind as old as language itself. The oeuvre and meaning of these poems is something we all share through our universal connectedness.

This book talks about love in many shades. Love is inherently erotic. The great Greek philosopher Plato once said, *"Eros is the greatest creative force in the universe."* I cannot agree more. I believe eros dwells in our innermost being as the spirit of creative expression. To me, eros is a great path that we must walk, a song we listen to, a game that we hunt and enjoy, a lesson to learn, a garden where flowers bloom, a prodigious puzzle to solve, a book to read, a chapter to write, and an ocean to swim in. That's what eros is to me.

Love is the true state of the human heart. When we love, we unguard our hearts. We open ourselves up to the world without any restraint. When passion flows, desires stir, our earthy senses become dull, and our ethereal self becomes illumined. At this stage, we are naked, totally naked, with little or no covering of ego.

Don't learn love;
   let love be what it is,
     simply:
your light, the wings of your soul,
the cosmic force, the music of the heart.
Love flows in;
   One does not choose to love.

Love is unique to each individual. Therefore the only way to speak about love is through poetry, since each poem is unique to each person who reads it. Through poetry we can glimpse the spirit of eros in its purest form. Poetry doesn't have to obey all the rules of language and conventional style; therefore much can be communicated. Where language fails, an image painted by words speaks volumes.

To love someone for the whole life
Is not easy.
It requires deep commitment.
That's why love is deep,
                    difficult,
                thrilling.
Such thrills are worth experiencing—
They make life worth living,
                and full of glee.

NAKED SOUL

THE EROTIC LOVE POEMS

A Garden of Love

They search for atonement and find it not.
They dig into the esoteric texts,
    memorize them,
    but do not see the garden.

They miss
    where the lovers are making love
    in a great union of ecstasy.

    They borrow ladders to put up
against the wall,
to peep into another world
    to have a glance of such nakedness,
    such passion.

The ladder breaks down,
the wall crumbles
under the heavy moans of lovers.

~

Bound For Me

She comes and looks deep
into my eyes
Her beautiful, majestic eyes
mesmerizing me
There she stands on the doorpost
waiting for my move
I take her hand into my hand
pressing softly

She takes off her clothes gently
to the last piece
There she stands in all skin
in all her glory
She offers me a rope and
stretches her arm
She is bound for me
there she waits for me

Warm
Exhilarating
lifting each other
Blindfolded warriors in a field
fingers
    tongue
        soft lips

Our weapons of love
and our bodies
    our shields

    She satisfies me in ways
my words fail
    I love her

~

SWEET ECSTASY

The ecstasy
  exploded
    within her.
She wanted to laugh,
  to cry,
  to scream out loud
At this perfect moment
  of climax;
  she was whole,
  she was alive—
It no longer mattered
If her eyes were
  open
    or
     closed.

~

JOURNEY OF LOVE

To all those who are love-sick:
Some cry, I want love; I need love!
I am loveless; pity on me;
Love me, love me, love me
PLEASE!
Oh dear, why don't you see!
Your eyes are closed to it.
Love is a breeze:
It moves the trees, sometimes just the leaves.
It can create waves in the ocean.
Love is whimsical and deep.

What will you give to your lover?
Do you possess a moonstone or stardust?
Have you planted a thousand roses?
Have you mapped the earth
To take your lover
On a journey full of mirth?

No—
    I don't have a moonstone,
       nor do I have stardust.
I am poor but have roses and flowers
    in all colors.

I will be kind to her limbs.
I can fill her life with passion.
Her organs will thank mine.
Her eyes will peck at mine.
Her hairs I will brush,
Igniting the passion in her soul,
Her vale merging with my knoll,
    A hummock
    just for her pleasures,
    ever waiting, ever desiring.

Your lover is there—
look, look, O young lover!
She is standing right behind you.

When will he make her an offer?
When will he be
    on the horse
    with a ring?

~

COME TO ME NAKED

Come when it's quiet
I like your way of moving
Slip into my
stillness
silence me

She emerges
    from her falling robe
I move closer and
    whisper

      let's stay inside
      lock the door
      come to me naked
      no one is here

It's time for us
    to become one
        between the sheets

~

GO KISS HER

Go kiss her from her forehead to her feet
Let this poor heart
    in you
    become courageous
Look how lovely, how lovely she is

Now you are ready, my friend
    now you know
You bring love with love
You make love with love
Love knows no desperation
Love knows no boundaries
    no limitation

You have charted the earth well
on the surface of her skin
with your beloved by your side
    hand in hand
    lips to lips
to the glorious birth
    of a new love

~

Your Hands That I Hold

Our souls, eternal companions
I will not let you wander anymore
My love, I am with you
Baby, every step that I tread
Is for us to come closer
Soul to soul

Your hands that I hold
I'll leave no more
Let me look into your soul
as you kiss my lips

As you hold my hand, my love
Fingers clasped—breast to breast
Your breathing over my face
breath to breath—we are one

Your soul that intoxicates me
day and night
Is also my life force
Without your life in my life
I am nothing
Just as without me in your life
You are nothing

~

THIS BLESSED LOVE

With all odds
    against us
Our heart in love
    is always young
Believing the impossible
Keeping the faith
    we made it
That's destiny

Finally hugging you
    kissing
        deeply
A friend, a lover
    my beloved
One human soul
    who I trust utterly
        This
    blessed love

~

Eternal Love

I secretly loved you for so long
My love
You gave me new life

Your deep, dark eyes
Made me drunk on our first trip to the wilderness
I wandered everywhere to seek solace
All I found was your sweet love
Echoing from the mountains
The valleys, the rivers, the trees

Our love was not of this world
Yes, it was sent from the stars
In the remote corners of our memories
Don't we still remember
    being with one another
        in a previous thousand lives?

I am not new to you
You are not new to me
I am here once again for you
Just as you came once again
    calling my name
    looking for that face
That heart that only beats for you

Do not ever leave me
We are two bodies but one soul
One cannot survive alone

How can we live without each other?
Love precedes all
We have come to this earth perhaps
    after thousands of years
Languishing, waiting for our return
In my shadow, your shadow dances
We live to uplift one another
We live to just love

There is no ending in such love
Only new beginnings
Tears flow boundlessly
Such is the beauty of this passion
The moments that we have shared
Our glory, our taste, our smell
Your skin and mine
Indistinguishable

~

FLOWERING OF INNER SELF

An explosion of soul
Flowering of inner self
Unleashing all that is within
confined
    and
        bounded

Anxious to merge with the infinite
the movements, motions, symbols
To merge in the silence
    the actions turning into joy

Love? How do I see it?
Let go of the self
    and you'll meet
a madman
    coming out of you

~

A Long Kiss

Clasping hands
Lifting her chin
Lost in each other's eyes
Midnight silence
A long kiss
Dawn breaks
Us apart

~

Taste of True Love

Do all you can to console me.
Make your words rich
As butter and chocolate.
Intoxicate me with your
Softest
    words.
Kiss and blow your heart
That I may touch your lips,
    Drunk
        under your love spell.

There are none like you.
Never have I felt
    this love before.
Your presence and kindest charm
    is hypnotic.
I am in deepest love with you,
Where passion burns every night,
Where I love
    every fiber of your being.

O soul of my soul,
I could die for you,
To see those eyes of yours
    and those sweet lips
Yielding immortal nectar,
    your puffy dollops.

I am never quite full
     drinking from your wetness.
Your juices and cum
     keep me satisfied,
But I wish
I could just drink them all night
     until forever,
Sweeping my tongue,
Smacking lips
     at your gushing door.
Its own language screams with passion—
     sup, sup, sup, sup,
The language of
     immortal love.

~

ENDLESS LOVE

Tonight our love is exposed
Starry nights, dancing trees
Seducing silence
How do I paint a love poem on you?

Every night I walked miles
Longing to catch my one delight
Every morning to leave you
A thank-you note

My darling dearest
My love to you is an eternal tale
Inexplicable, mystifying, delicious
Let us write each page together

~

My Lover Is Sly

My lover is shy;
She would not let me touch her.
I wrote poems to her;
They fell silent on the paper.

My lover is sly,
She would tape us together,
Reading my longings, my desires,
Playing to my fulfillment.

Moaning,
    Groaning,
Bound together, glued,
Holding our hands together;
One strong fragrance
Holding our breath together;
Silent climatic death,
    Sweet ecstasy.

~

OUR SACRED DANCE

Love as pure
Like little children
    Running around, restless
So naive at heart
    And hands
        Without blame

Don't come
    And try to stop us
That we celebrate
Our sacred dance
In our preserved innocence
    Tonight

~

FROZEN MOMENT

The night is long
    but the hours
        short
We take turns

The friction from our
    skin
Causes us to
    sweat

This frozen moment
    in time
        eternal
Two bodies
    love dreams

~

A New Beginning

When my friends ask
about you
I tell them
    that I met you today
My friends marvel at this
    But to me
        You are a new
beginning
        every day

There is no end in such love
Nothing is old here
    We age
but our spirit remains the same
and we become
    the part of eternal sky

~

In The Open

Bathe me
in the sunshine
Let the wild air
    touch my skin
Swim in my
    presence
naked and free
    Love me

~

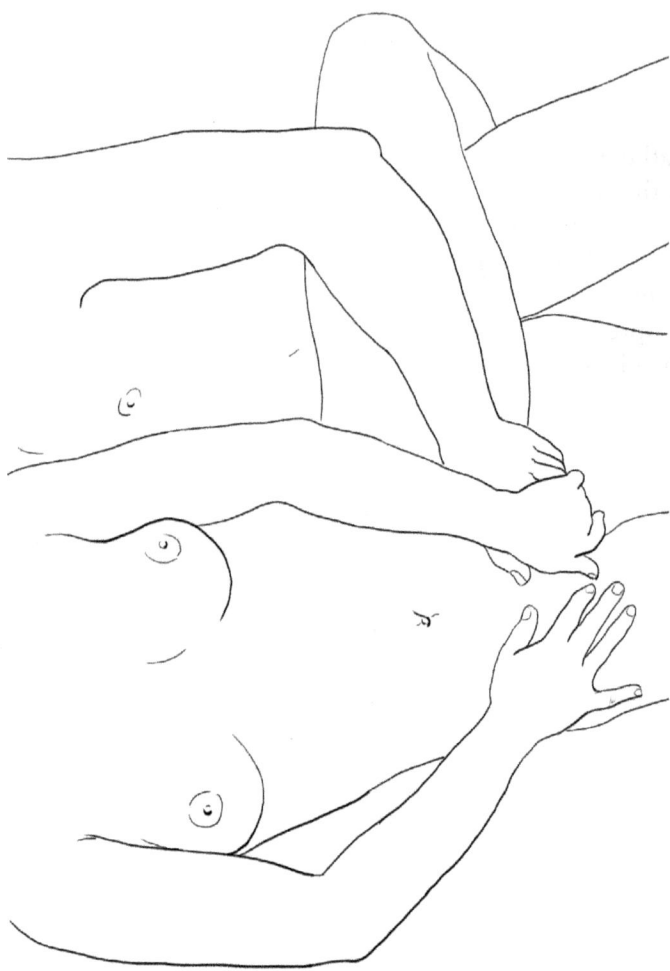

Let Me Touch You

Squeeze
Rub
Fingers or feathers
    Burning fire
        Quenching water
Whither, O whither!
       None would suffice but me
Her

~

FLYING WITH YOUR LOVE

Lovey, I am flying far away with your love,
Floating miles away with your picture in my heart.

It is a bit cold without the warmth of your hug;
I am starving for your delicious lips
and the sweet, honeyed kiss.

The sun is setting and the moon is rising;
The clouds are gliding and the wind playing.

I am flying away, far away from the sun and the moon,
Across the ocean, over the deep, blue sea.

I have left my heart filled with love for you,
My presence as the sun, moon, and wind to kiss you.

~

Touch Me Anywhere

Outside a night club:

Are we going to your house?
Sounds dreamy.
You were amazing tonight.
Can you keep a secret?

Outside a quiet house:

Tonight feels like a dream.
Want to come in?
I think you can use a drink.
"Sexy lady—that'll work."

Inside the living room:

Can I ask you something?
I want to probe deep
Inside your mysterious heart,
But first let me change quickly.

Naked on the door:

Want to take bath together?
You are so handsome.
I can't believe I am living this.
Tonight you can touch me anywhere.

~

RED HOT

Red dress, cherry lips
Dark glasses
White pearly neckless

Summer day, hot sun
Juice in hand
You walked in

Sexy swinging hips
red heels
Hypnotic music of footsteps

Gusty afternoon
Swirling red skirt
Enticing red lingerie

Silk, lacy, seductive
Soft and feminine
Begging for an opening

Changing room
By the poolside
You took them off

My heart beating faster
Anticipating thrill
Can't wait to say *Hi*

You took notice of me
I took notice of your
racy see-through bikini

Dark nipples
Fluffy, pointed, edible
Lipstick shape

Round curvy bottom
Mango-shaped breasts
Salacious invitation

In the water
Deep sweet kisses
To the room

~

OUR SOULS IN LOVE

Let's find a secluded trail
    and get lost in the woods;
Let our bodies unite
    as trees merge in a forest.

Let us be so close,
    our souls fused in love
Like floating sticks in the river,
    two hearts coalesced as one.

~

LONELY BEACH

White sands
    on your body
Shape of a heart
      on your bum
Summer hotness
What do I have here?
    wet
        tropical
         juice
Waiting to be tasted

Take off
your
    pants
Let me pull up
    my skirt
There is no one
watching
on this
    lonely beach

~

YOUR SWEET MUFFIN

You feel shy but then
    you throw kisses at me
My love, you surely stop my heartbeat
I want to get lost in you
Look at your toned legs
Are they hiding something?
No, they reveal and entice
Pushing out that inviting shape so clearly visible
An avocado
    Or something juicier

I can't wait to hold you in my arms
    and deeply suck, kiss
        your fluffy muffin
A thousand and one times
    until
        you scream in pleasure

~

SOUL TO SOUL

Love me
    for my mind,
my heart, my being
Don't worry about my body
I can give you sex
    any second
But to love you back
    I must first feel
        soul-to-soul love

~

DIPPED IN WINE

Cucumber dipped in wine
In your mouth
Then a strawberry
To that sweet taste
Sweet, salty, sourly
And I shall bring
Banana. Pepper. Carrot. Zucchini
There, to put, to eat
Until we are full

~

DIVINELY SEXY

I want you
    to make love
to me
Kiss me, seduce me
Make love to me
    everywhere
Until
    I just fall on my knees

And let me worship
    your each part
Waiting
       to viciously devour
    your frilly pink pie
Your face now has
That look
    So divinely sexy
       Or call it
        devilishly seductive

~

Devour Me

Devour me in all places
On ground, walls, bed

Fill me hard
with all you have
I will lick
your fingers in my mouth

Take your fruit out
I will eat it
while resting on my four limbs

Then bring it out
And put it in
Until it floods
    Our souls

~

EVERLASTING LOVE

Our love is like a new spring
A colorful fall
Like warm summer nights
Beauty of winter snow and ice
Everlasting,
    Perennial

~

So Sexy

She is
putting nail polish
On her toes
With cotton pads in between
    fingers
Gently moving arms
Painting the art
    with that naked brush
Giving away the smell
Of deep nostalgia
    Of time
when we took
    our first shower together
    and came to bed
with burning lust

Tonight
    the wait
        When she is just watching
    her feet
        for the nail paints to dry

You can tell
    What is going on
        in her mind

~

Sexy Little Things

Your cute face
Your loving presence
In a million years
    I would not want to make you sad
    not for a moment

Today
I just want to spend with you
    cuddling and caressing

~

LOVE SEES NOTHING

Love accepts and does not analyze
Love surrenders, does not resist
Love sees without eyes
    It hears without words
    It understands the silence
Love communes direct
      and deeper

~

FORBIDDEN LOVE

We think of prayer
    while making love,
Meditating on the celestial.
    Our house is a temple,
    a sacred place
    where I burn incense,
chant, sing, and dance
With my beloved,
Our souls offering our best,

    Worshipping
        like
            mad priests.

~

DO THAT AGAIN

Freshly fucked
lying on the green

In the garden
you took the feather
out from your hair
and handed it to me

To play it on your soft skin
as I moved it over your body
with your back arched
and eyes closed

goose bumps

We both knew we weren't finished

Make love to me again
once more
fuck me

~

Love Marks

You come in broad daylight
To make love to me
To get a refreshing taste
And leave
    with an unfinished story

At night
You pour yourself on me
    Your sticks like fingers
        Your chain like arms
          Wrapping around me
        Leaving
          its love marks

~

LONGING

We met and saw each other
We hugged and rubbed our nose
Cheek to cheek

We talked for hours
Her lips got dried and mine pale
We approached closer

face to face
lips to lips
breath to breath

She was satisfied
And I filled
Our lips wet, moist, and red

~

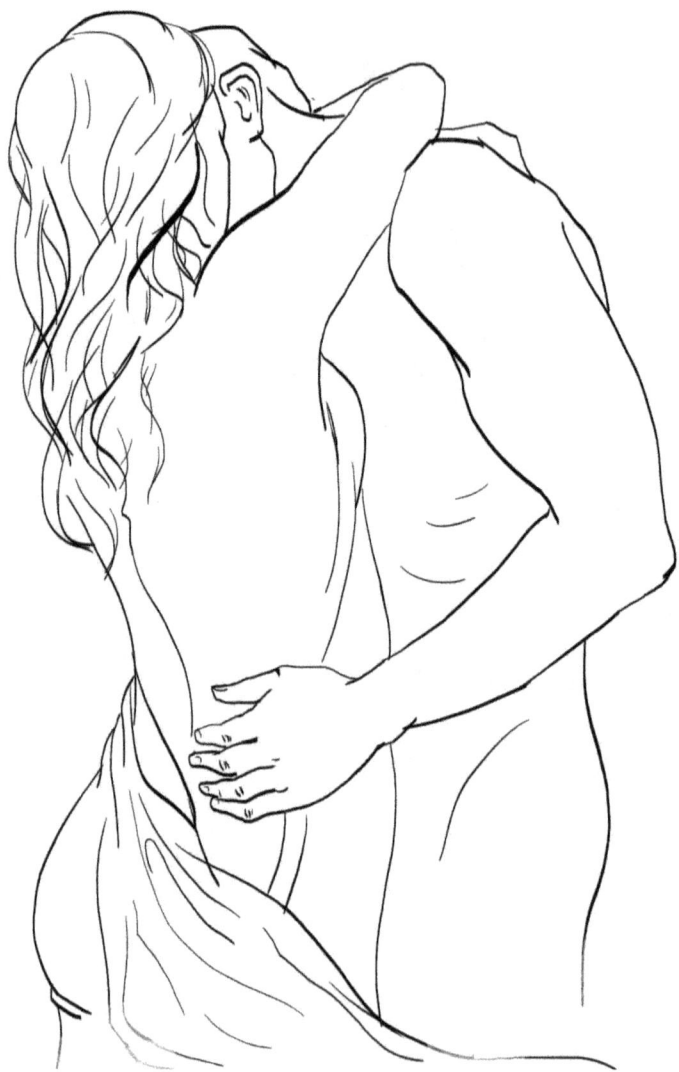

BEAUTY OF TRUE LOVE

Having trust
    in intimacy
        is tremendously
romantic
As a morning rainbow
    reaches
        the fountain
So is the beauty
        of true love

~

FOOLISHNESS OF LOVE

He who watches the beauty,
He who believes in love
    is never aloof,
        never detached.

Our logic ridicules this love,
and my heart smiles knowingly
    at the foolishness
        of thoughts.

~

POETIC LAND

Take me away to your poetic land
Where we can get lost in each other,
Where the milestones are all paved with love—
A journey filled with lust,
The sound of the surroundings
enchanted with your kiss!

Take me away to your poetic land
Where we'll make things steamy,
We'll make things sweet;
Where we'll breathe for each other,
Taste each other deeply;
Where we'll make the world envious
with our moment of bliss!

~

Coming Home

Coming home
such a delight
Lady of my dreams
    cooking
All naked but
    an apron
Her flesh giving away
the aroma of
    freshly cooked food

I hug her from behind
    Her tits pointed
aroused
I gently whisper into her ear
    "I love you"
        As I take off
my clothes.

~

A WILD MOONLIT NIGHT

I walked hurriedly to her home
On a wild moonlit night
She is in her inner chamber
Painting a picture of us
Naked brush, naked canvas, naked mind
On a moonlit gusty night

There she stands
At the corner of the wooden window
Holding hands with her shadow
I approached gently toward her
Only to discover
That the shadow is mine

~

KISSES

Slowly and soft
Playing, laughing, experimenting
Relaxed and happy
Then passionately and long
Cheeks, lips, jaw, neck, and lips again
Deep and sucking
Forehead to the belly button
Behind the neck to bump down

Rubbing nose and cheeks
Pressing lips
Fondling breasts and butt
Cuddling with ears
Embracing eyes, looking shy
Spices of variety
Bare skin
A touch of sensation
Against a wall, on the ground
Or in my hands, over me, into each other
Tightly locked, so soothing
A spider web
Searching hands, unexplored regions
Wet and moist

Taking a break
Doing it all over again
and again
    and again
Until
    the morning rushes upon us

~

A GREAT PUZZLE

From the top of her long, silky hairs
To her beautiful, sun-licked, shining face
To the tip of her soft, curved breasts
To midway between her sweet, warm thighs
To the bottom of her long, strong feet
She is one great puzzle
A great treasure to be hunted
A mystery to be admired
A land to be explored
A journey to be undertaken

~

POETRY OF KISSING

In the poetry of kissing
There is no right way to kiss
No two are exactly the same
Boundless, this art of kissing
Sometimes deeper
Other times just the lips

Holding it longer and shorter
Together laughing about it
Variety is the added hot spice
Tenderly sucking your partner's lips
Take a deep breath
    and
        break
To delicately
        compliment her

~

KISSING YOU

Kissing you:
Feelings immense,
Irresistible,
Crazy, warm, cozy,
Soft, sensual, passionate,
Romantic,
Inexorable,
Slow,
Willfully sinking,
An instance of being intimate.
Tasty and juicy, our sensations progress,
Salacious arousal,
That moment of touch of feelings,
Intense sense of the lesser-known organs.
Our hands roam and get caught up in the search,
An instance of being intimate,
Unexplainable, savorinesses indescribable,
Something that has to be known by oneself.
Such are you my beloved,
Such is your love.

~

WALK OVER ME

Your feet on my back
A sun embracing the planets
My spine feels its warmth
Skin rubbing skin
Fading, the separateness
Of our beings

Your walk over me
Strengthening each of my cells
Your joyous laughter
And my mild smile
Begets an atmosphere of ecstasy
This moment

~

IF YOU WERE

If you were an eagle
Soaring high
And I were the valley,
Would you come down to feast?

If you were a blooming flower,
Purple, red, and yellow,
And I the earth beneath,
Would you ever touch me?

If you were the sun
Shining brightly
And I a tree in the forest,
Would you rise to give me warmth?

If you were the waters
In the rivers and in the clouds
And I was just a barren desert,
Would you ever rain on me?

If you were a mighty ocean
With all the turbulent waves
And I a lonely boat amid them,
Would you ever sink me down?

~

DEAR LOVE

Dear love, to you, what love can I bring?
A fountain to fill your cup
A flute to let pass your breath
A bed sheet to comfort you
A bird to fly and sing with you
But suffer not my eyes and my lips
To hunger for your face
And in thirst for your well
My heart cries in joy to you
I love you, O my beloved

Let countless years pass by and end
I can be a wave and you an endless ocean
A searching bee and you the flower garden
A lowly blade of grass and you the green valley
A faint shade and you the shining lamp
A sweet memory and you the soul possessing it
I don't know my love's own depth
Just that this foolish, silly love
Has no beginning and no end
I love you, O my beloved

~

My Love Within

You are the candle of my eternal soul
Its radiant flame of first, true love.

What is in my heart
can be only seen through caring eyes
and be only known through my breath
No one knows what I possess within
Oh what pain I do endure
to hide my fervor, love, within

Oh what joy, oh what agony
this, the language of gentle love
which can be only sensed and felt
can be only given
    and
        gained

~

HER FLYING KISS

The whole night
I take turns in sleep
    Right and left
    On my back and sides again

A gentle breeze passes
over my face and body
It is my beloved's song,
    Her flying kiss

~

First Smooch Kiss

The first smooch kiss
A spring night
Moonlit pastoral lake
Dancing elm, oak, and pear
Mild breeze
Courting song of crickets and katydid
Secrecy and silence
Standing close, smiling, and stirring
Our necks tilted on the right
One hand behind and one front
Thumbs caressing the face
And fingers
    releasing the locks of your hair

Our hands massaging behind and front
The adorable landscape of love
Bump and breasts
Belly and waist
Crossed legs
Delirious smell of the skin
Taste of your rosy lips and sweet saliva
The taste of one another
Outer eyes closed, inner open
My upper lip between your lips
Your lower lip between mine

Rubbing, pressing, sucking, kissing
Small and big, short and long
Goose bumps and blushing
Breathtaking, timelessness, breathless
Uncaptured, indefinable moment!

~

You Ignited A Fire

Last time we met and gazed at one another
You ignited a fire
and left!

You went away to your business
Leaving this poor soul in misery and longing

You ignited a fire
and left!

I waited for you until darkness
You came late and found me unconscious
The pain was so intense, dear
What else could I have done?

You ignited a fire
and left!

Just by your one touch I was revived
Putting my face to your breast
Crying like an infant, I sobbed

You ignited a fire
and left!

You went away to your business!

~

RED MOON

When the long day ends
And the bashful evening comes with the moon
Your memory then arrives
And my heart cries in secret aching for you
O my love, I love you

~

CHERRY BLOSSOM

I wanted you so long
I always sang this song

You came along in autumn
I bloomed like a cherry blossom

Your presence put me in awe
I was out of all my senses

Your magnetic force
    pulled me close
to your gravity of love

You smiled and came closer
I could not stop
    myself to be yours

You teased me everywhere
with your fingers
    we had some sweet giggles

Your lips so soft
your body so attractive
We made love
    I felt that even if I die
        I am still alive

~

True Love

The arousing emotional fiber of first love
An exhilarating love at first sight
A bittersweet painful passion
An overwhelmingly deep love
Gentle as a summer gust
Fierce and chilling as the ice cliffs
That is the way your love is to me
Universal as life itself

~

THIS IS ALL I DO NOW

I look for your face wherever I go
Whenever I close my outer eyes
    Only you I see
    Only you I feel
I am bewildered and mad in this love

Catching your eye
    Writing you letters
    Bathing your body
    Sending you flowers
This is all I do now

~

SOUL MATE

It is in love that this world makes sense
It is in love, this life's essence
My soul mate, O my love, my friend
Together our lives now securely blend

We are together in our joys and grief
In this journey of meadows and of peaks
O soul mate, what a mystery unknown
To us that in this deeper love is shown

~

ONE SOUL

We should meet as if
We have never met before
Then depart as if not departed
What a mystery
One soul
Two bodies
Whispering the songs of love
Into each other's ears

~

COME NAKED

In this river of wine
    I love my love with love
        Never known before

Don't walk into this river of hope
    wearing a robe
You don't take a good bath
    wearing your gown
Come naked
In this garden
Without clothes, without figs

I am glad
    that you found me
How pure a flame now burns
This thirst
    with which I burn

∼

LOVE FANTASIES

The heart-shaped, red, hanging lights on our wall;
I see you in your full existence,
with all your pure skin,
all naked, with all your appeal.
The shiny, silky-smooth skin all bright and red;
I sense you, I touch you to devour
the deliciousness in you.
I come closer, dripping your body with my wet hair;
I suck in your honeycomb;
I taste the sweetness.
My honey, oh so sweet.
Your honey, oh, sweet honey—it's one of a kind.
I drink it—all drunk with full pleasure, I feel total ecstasy.
Then I ride like a cowgirl to reach as far as I can be.
I hustle, I shake, I grind, I wind, I go deep
where there is only one path and only one way to be.
This road is an endless road; miles away it can lead.
It will be the road where you will find me,
and I will be riding on it endlessly!

~

ONE, TWO

One bed
    Two lovers

One pillow
    Two heads
    Two minds
One thought

One blanket
    Two pair of legs
    Two bodies
One heart

        Two tongues
        One kiss

~

WAIT FOR ME

Wait for me
Eyes closed, dancing
   to the rhythm of eros
Where heart and heart meet
    where the soul
    dances with the soul
There
      then

A deeper closeness emerges
All unknowns become known

We bloom into the darkness
Merged with existence
Experiencing the totality of the whole

    Into the beautiful coming

      ~

MAKHMAL AND KASTOORI

Two lovers meet
One day, in secrecy

Hearts warm as a pillow
of *makhmal*

The lover says to his love
"You are a pearl buried in the
ruins of the world
People come and go
they watch
But they cannot smell the *kastoori*
They laugh, eat, and joke with you
But they don't see your heart"

The mirror slips from her hand
It falls down
She cries and with shivering hand
She says
Tear apart the wall
You'll not need any windows anymore

makhmal: velvety leaves
kastoori: musk

~

PICNIC SEX

Holding hands
 Kissing in public
Giving sexy looks
  Holding each other close
   Walking arm in arm
    Naked in the woods
    Picnic sex

~

You Mean Everything

The innocent
Smile
    of your face, darling
is more luminous
    than ten thousand suns
Your one smile
    is worth
        the whole world
Your love
        has driven me
    insane
And

to tell you
    all my pains
    all my love
is a gift of love
    far too expensive
    Your presence
        means
          everything

~

A PERFECT EVENING

Night comes slowly
I am anxious to meet you
Your lights are still on
I wander outside in the moonlight

You walk out
In a flowing gown
Turquoise
Just perfect for this night

The moon gives enough sight
For me to watch your eyes
I hand you a wrapped surprise
You kiss me in return

Touching and yearning for
each other in a loving way
Kissing when people aren't looking
We walk away
from your home

~

FIERY CREATURES

Embracing your body close,
Holding you tight with my warm hug,

The warmth of your body
heat in the air all around as fog,

The burning fire in our senses
All ready to consume us.

Our bodies dancing and rubbing,
Tossing each other zig and zag—

It feels magical; it feels mystical;
all of it,
all of us,
    under the love rug,
Fiery creatures in the dark.

~

SEDUCTION

Him:
Do you want to share my ice cream
play footsie?
Inch by inch
I'll climb up
You eat

Her:
I want to go horseback riding
By candlelight
With a bottle of wine
squeezing with my thighs
I want a stallion

~

NAKED BATH

At first
I saw you
in a public fountain
    bathing
A body so complete

I melted immediately in your love
This enchanting alchemy
I became ensnared by you
Wanting to adore you, my love
    in secret and in silence

Come follow me tonight
In the moonlight
By the river
Leave your clothes on the bank
I will teach you romance
I will show you love.

~

I Love It

I love it
When you hold me
   From behind

With your hands caressing
my back, holding
   Where it is tiniest

I am thrilled
As you throw me on the bed
   And press on me

On the wall
I see your dark shadow
   Riding a horse

You move your fingers
Up and down
   Rubbing my pear-shaped bum

When you kiss me
On my neck
   Your hands squeezing my breasts

I love it
I absolutely love it
    Scream my exaltations.

~

WAKE UP

You tickle me
In early morning
And gently whisper
  Wake up
Into my ears

You slide me down
Into the wetness
    Even before
    I am awake

~

MORNING LOVE

You make a tent of
   blanket
   to cover my face
   from the morning sun
and watch me breathe

When I move or growl
you kiss me with a smile
All this time
while I am still dreaming
you already know
what you are making
for breakfast

You gently stroke my body
With the feeling of a new touch
You don't wake me up
but arouse me from my sleep
Caressing gently all over
you hug me close to your
heart
   We make love
   Even before we wake up
        for the day

~

STANDING GLORY

Fingers move
On his
    naked ribcage
And I get to see
    what I need
Standing straight

~

SOUND OF WETNESS

At first glance,
it won't slide.
Then, the
sound of wetness
proves me wrong.

Early morning,
our neighbors are awakened
to the song of
two love birds.

~

CUDDLE NAKED

We cuddle naked
On a lonely island, in the sea,

Where our bodies press each other
On the sand, under the tree.

With sound of splashing waves,
Your arms tangle me, legs ready to heave.

Where we make love to each other,
My body under yours, we are so free.

~

BEAUTY BEYOND WORDS

Let the king come to the bride's chamber
And charm all her friends and chambermaids.
Let the princess walk to the knight's castle
And mesmerize all the guards and pickets.
O where such beauty, lo, where such fate,
When our will is feeble and our love so faint

~

Tonight I Want

Tonight
I want to make love with you
With chocolate and cream
I want to rub
I want to eat my fill
Until my goddess feels
She has been worshiped
fully
Tongue whirling
    turning your ripe pussy
into the temple of
sweet sensual fragrance
topped with cream

~

HOLD MY FIRE

I pleaded to her
Please don't judge my heart, my darling
I am the same yesterday and today
    and will be forever
The changes you'll see in me are not me
They are my body wearing different robes
But within, I am eternally yours

In my soul, in my heart
I am the same, unchanging
I am awakened by your flower-like lips
and
    touched by your mysterious love
What remains of me now is only a garden
    of sweet kisses
In this renewal, the veils have been torn
My heart is burning and my love warm
My contemplative mind has vanished
The nectar of this love is bewildering me
All opposites are united
When I kiss the honey-soaked tongue of my lover
Her body perfumed, arousing me with just a touch
I'll hold your fire forever
In this serenity of love

~

CRAZY LOVE

Few are those who
are the mad lovers
Praising their love
in front of others
I love to kiss her leg
While placing her feet in my lap
Gently massaging them
While we wait for our food

Even before the food arrives
　　She whispers, *I am so wet,*
My beloved prince
I want just the two of us alone
Unleash your inner fire
　　and burn me in your passion
You know what I want
　　for food
　　　　To eat

~

I Love You Like No Other

Singing, dancing, musing
Love, Love, Love
Unimaginable joy
Annihilated in this sacred play
   …bewildered,
I explode in ecstasy
I love you
   Like no other lover

~

I SEE YOU

I lean to kiss you
    with the excitement
    of first attempt
My heart burning
    with passion and lust

In the exchange of kisses
I'm already aroused
My eyes are closed
But I see you
    in my mind
You are so beautiful!

~

DEPTH OF MY LOVE

Oh what a beautiful
moment it is,
Eyes overwhelmed
by the serene, exquisite
    beauty of nature.

Mind full of thought of love,
How lovely it is,
the luscious rainforest
    like your existence, always evergreen.

Oh how lovely is the
    clear blue sky,
endless horizon miles across;
How deep it is,
the clear blue sea,
    like the depth of my love.

~

New Love

There is the same moon outside the hut
The windows and the hole in the roof
Bring the same moonlight
But all rays look different
Some shaded, some bright
Some make shadows; some come as beams of arrows
The same sun rises and sets down in the west
As the earth revolves in madness
Spinning like a drunken dancer
But no two mornings and evenings are the same
No two stars look the same each night
No two breezes are one
So is my love
Every night is a new life
A new love song

~

SLOW SUNSET

Slow sunset
     Red sky, gray clouds
       Birds flying back home
         Holding hands together
      Rapt and spellbound
     Two lovers
   Becoming one and
The same

~

ECSTATIC LOVE

In this ecstatic love
All my actions
have become
    effortless
My body moves to help
And my hands grasp, stretch, and cling
Fulfilling
    their
        own desires

~

LOVE PRAYER

This I pray, my dearest love,
Mold me, God, in this sacred love
Help me to expand my heart;
 give me the strength and courage;
 give me the embracing arms,
 greater love,
 bigger sacrifices,
 deeper ecstasy
Eternally

~

TRUE ROMANCE

Money can buy some rice wine
But not a true romance
Wealth can blind some shallow eyes
But can't win an excellent lady's hand
Character, virtues, and patience
Soaked with true love and kindness
Will alone cause two souls
To be friends and lovers forever

~

TO GIVE MY ALL

At last a soul to whom to give my all
A love song like a prayer call
A face ultimately to behold forever
A name to sing and leave never

A match who reflects me and I her
A graceful echo, soul's inner myrrh
A special lover, my wait is over
At last a soul to dwell within and cover

~

SEX IN THE CITY

It is February
From my balcony
Yesterday I saw
a man in suit and tie
eating his lunch in a Mercedes
some old ladies crossing the street
in colorful hats
Maybe they were from England
A group of Jews with beards
and long coats walked slowly

"Let them mind their business,
while we have sex in the city"
Said she
    and we took our clothes off
All this time
amid the noise and mayhem
We made love
    culminating in syrupy peace

~

I WISH

I wish you were with me
tonight, here, right now
Wish you came to eat with me
while there was still some food left

Everywhere, everyplace
I miss you
Ever since I first saw you smile
at me
I have lost my own laughter
Now I just look for you
Everywhere
Even though I know
You live in my heart

I still wish
You came out tonight
Your food is getting cold

~

You Collect All

Your loving touch
over my face with your fingers,
while my legs touch your cold feet,
Giving warmth to my heart.
As I come
You collect all
that comes out
and put it on your breasts
And then you say,
now let me come on top,
    now spread your legs.

~

HOW TO MAKE LOVE TO ME

Touch me softly
And run a feather
From over my neck to my belly

Then
Up and down
round and round
Move your hands gently
Over my boomerang

And when you can't hold it
Anymore
Move fast and slow
Eye to eye
Until our faces glow red
and our hair is wet with sweat

Crisscross, our
legs like scissors

~

MOON LOVER

Frozen in glacial ice
You shine in the starlight
In silence
With the warmth of the sun
You flow
To your freedom
Leaving the moon and the dark night
behind you

They mourn and grieve
Finding you not
The following night

You come and shower
Your love
Scattering your misty eyes
From above the clouds
Circling the mountain
A mystic river

You yet again flow
Leaving the saddened rocks
behind
and merge into the ocean

From where
You ascend to paradise
And make love with the moon and stars
Above the glacial ice
Silently smiling
Dark nights

~

THINKING ABOUT YOU

I will be
    the first warmth of sun
Kissing you tenderly
    hugging you tightly
I will be kissing you
    with that soft breeze
till dusk

I will be
watching your movements
from the
    desperate
      bright moon

I will be
    thinking about you
      in my silence
My heart will sing for you
    wishing for your good health
      praying
        for our
      Endless love

~

I Yearn To Consume You

As lovers in my dreams we meet
With every breath I feel you
My heart yearns to see you again
No other treasure I seek

My heart breaks
at the memory of your smile
The endless pools of your dark eyes
your touch, your taste
your sensuality
I yearn to consume you

~

I Wait For You

I wait
    by an empty garden
        for you
To walk together
    hand in hand
The beauty of our bond
    far beyond
    the flowers around us
Our companionship
    blossoming
        into
fruits of the night

I will be waiting
    My sweet love
my hero, my soul mate
To give
    my love
in abundance
every moment
    and
        every day

~

COME TO ME NOW

In you I find my childhood friend
Leaving you is thirsting without water
Kissing the locks of your hair
    I am bewildered
by your magnificent beauty

Your heart, your juicy lips
    are my consoling towers
The depth and tranquility in your eyes
    are pools
from which I dare not escape

My heart longs for you, searches for you
The shining sun is not bright enough
The moon moans at my pitiful provisions
My angel,
    please don't leave me breathless

O wild, willowy, naughty, nimble
    Don't tease me anymore
Tantalized and mesmerized I am
    Come to me now and make love

~

SECRET SONGS AND PRAYERS

O my love
Look into my eyes; what do you see?
I see only us in our eyes
There is no boundary to keep us constrained
We are eternally free
We are free birds and we serve only the heavens
As I listen to you and you listen to my beats
Our voices echo across the oceans
For eons to come, such passion will be remembered
So is our love, my sweetheart

This love
    You have seen within yourself
    You have felt its power
    You have dreamed of the future
    You have written secret songs
        and
Prayers

~

SANCTUARY

I no more hear the noises
This all has become so sweet
I no more see the pain
You raised me up from the dead

My love, in your dancing beauty
I am charmed and captured
This is not a fairytale, not a dream

In your invitations for love
Clinging to your silent wings
I see the promises of hope

I belong to you, O Love
Like the first day of spring
I sing all hymns to hope
You are my home and refuge

~

My Love Brings Me Joy

Oh, I just want to kiss you, dear.
We spoke not for the whole day.
Nothing seems calm; all appears uneasy.
My breath is short; my tongue is sour.
Oh, my heart only desires for you.
It cries for you from within me.

Who knows how it feels,
crying without tears,
eating without wine?
My strides are waste;
the dreams are empty—
I see the whole earth waste.
Only my love brings me joy.

~

YOUR PRESENCE

Wishing to kiss you
    I leaned
but
    You were gone
Even though
    your body was not here
I could still embrace you
    in my soul

With a heart
full of passion
we made
    deathless
    love—
        us together
wild and untamed
    no desire restrained

~

HOT FUG

I wander no longer
I prefer to wait at my master's chamber
 To eat
 To drink
 To talk of love
He flames my heart
 With desire
 Never felt before
Enthralled and awestruck
 I lose my senses
 In
His love
All night long
I am consumed
 In a hot passion

Don't ask!
 I don't
 Know
 We ever sleep or endlessly frig
 Can I even count?

~

ONLY PRAYER

May the God of mercy have mercy on us
May we sense each other's heart and needs
May such a day never come
    when we have to doubt or judge one another
        and may we walk together, parallel
    always, forever, till death and beyond
    hand in hand, heart to heart
This relationship will only add to our quality of life
Not subtract from it
Every fiber of our being may fall in love
    with one another
Making us both
Human and divine

~

BLOW HOT BREATH

Your soft lips to all my lips
    blow hot
        breath everywhere
Your tongue to my tongue
        taste me
        everywhere
Your fiery desires to fulfill all my desires
        cry out loud
        love fountains everywhere

~

Finale In Your Room

You pull me closer
    with your magical love
    like a magician
    doing his brilliant magic

I give up, disappear,
    lose my mind
    as if I am yours, for
    finale in your room

~

INDEX OF FIRST LINES

GRATITUDE

I would like to thank Nikki Siclari and Alicia Cole for the time and effort they put into the editing of this book. Without having these wonderful and exceptionally qualified editors on my team, I could not have brought this book to fruition.

Special thanks are also due to Chandan Saurabh for creating the beautiful illustrations for the book.

I express my sincere thanks to you, O dear friends, whom I cannot mention by name because you are so many. Missing any one of you would be an injustice. But I mean you all. Thank you.

Also, I cannot express my thanks in mere words toward all of you dear and lovely readers. Without you, this book would mean very little. I wish you good fortune in love and matters of the heart. May your life be full of passion and a continually evolving, happy journey.

Salil Jha

NAKED SOUL BLOG

The Naked Soul website and blog, **www.nakedsoulpoems.com**, is a valuable resource for poetry lovers, writers, explorers, artists, and anyone who is interested in reading good, authentic words. The blog is designed as a knowledge bank full of sweet things of life, deep thoughts, traveling tips, and helpful how-to articles.

Do visit us frequently and start or join a conversation. Love, Peace, Namaste.

GET YOUR FREE GIFT

Receive a surprise gift.

All you have to do is take a selfie with this book and (*a*) post it on the Naked Soul's Facebook page, or (*b*) post it on Instagram with the hashtag #nakedsoulpoems, or (*c*) tweet it with the hashtag #nakedsoulpoems and mention @nakedsoulpoems.

If you bought this book online, please leave a review. It helps both the author and the book you love.

All winners will be randomly picked. This is an evergreen promotion, and therefore there is no end date to participate and WIN. We want to see you and surprise you.

ABOUT THE AUTHOR

Salil Jha, born in India, is a contemporary poet and transpersonal coach with a unique style of writing. His poems explore themes of passionate love, universal truths, and human beings' inner longing. Known for its visual narrative of the sensual and mystical experiences in love, Salil Jha's poetry has explored emotions from the purely erotic to the purely spiritual.

Salil spends most of his time writing and traveling, although he does occasionally do public speaking and poetry reading at conferences and events. For more information you can contact him on his blog. Salil lives in Boston, Massachusetts, and frequently blogs on www.nakedsoulpoems.com.

Connect with Salil on:
    www.nakedsoulpoems.com.

Instagram: @Naked_Soul_Poems
Facebook: Naked Soul: The Erotic Love Poems
facebook.com/lovepoemsseries
Pinterest: pinterest.com/Naked_Soul
Twitter: @NakedSoulPoems
Google+: Naked Soul Poetry